Flamingo

Royal
Tern

Limpkin

Adélle
Penguin

Ruffed
Grouse

Western Grebe

Cardinal

Cliff
Swallow

Ruby-throated
Hummingbird

While her eggs hatch, a cautious mother ostrich stands guard.

# Baby Birds
## and How They Grow

By Jane R. McCauley

BOOKS FOR YOUNG EXPLORERS
NATIONAL GEOGRAPHIC SOCIETY

Look! An eggshell is cracking. A chicken is ready to hatch. With a special tooth on its beak, the tiny chick turns round, chipping at its shell. Cheep! Cheep! it cries.

After several hours, it pushes apart its shell and wiggles out. The chick is tired. It must rest and dry out. When it is a day old, it looks very different. The fuzzy chick can run about and feed itself. But for a while, it will stay close to its mother.

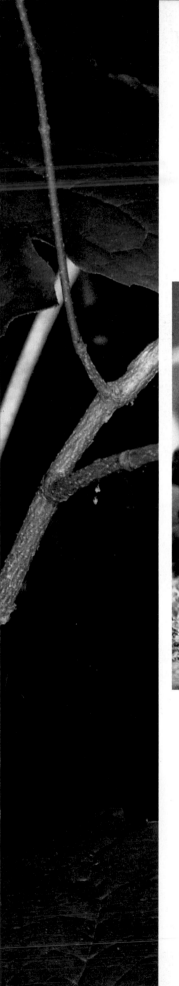

Birds live everywhere. If you look up in the trees, around you on the ground, and out on the water, you will see many different kinds of birds.

GREAT WHITE PELICAN

At first, many young birds are helpless. Their parents must keep them warm and make sure they have enough food. Cheeping loudly, a baby warbler opens its beak wide. The parent drops food into its mouth. A hungry baby pelican reaches into the pouch under its parent's bill. There the adult pelican holds some food for the baby.

HOODED WARBLER

LAUGHING GULL (ABOVE), WESTERN GREBE (OPPOSITE)

Often adult birds must protect their babies. A bird called a western grebe looks as if it might be wearing a black hat. While the mother swims about, the baby grebe stays safe and snug just under her wing. A gull shades its young from the hot sun with its long tail. Terns warn another gull to keep away from their chick by flapping their wings and screeching.

ROYAL TERN

HERRMAN'S GULL

MUTE SWAN

Soon after hatching, certain kinds of birds can almost take care of themselves. Baby geese, called goslings, follow their parents to the water. They can already swim. The baby swan knows how to clean its feathers. The young killdeer feed themselves. Still, the mother is sure to be nearby.

KILLDEER (ABOVE), SNOW GOOSE (BELOW)

Peekaboo! A ruffed
grouse chick is hiding
among some leaves. The
grouse often lives near
forests, where it builds its
nest on the ground.

The baby grouse leaves
the nest soon after
hatching. At first
it cannot fly; but the
colors of its feathers
blend with the leaves
and help protect it. If
an enemy comes near,
the tiny bird stays very
still. Then it is hard to see.

RUFFED GROUSE

10

GREAT HORNED OWL (ABOVE), WOOD DUCK (BELOW), RED-TAILED HAWK (OPPOSITE)

A red-tailed hawk flaps its wings as it walks about on its nest. Soft fluffy feathers, called down, cover the bird. Later, mature feathers will develop.

An owl stretches its wings. Can you see the long feathers on the owl's wings? They are called flight feathers. Birds need such feathers to be able to fly. A wood duck rapidly beats its wings. Birds must have strong muscles to move their wings. When their muscles are strong enough and their feathers are long enough, the young birds will fly.

This robin is too young to fly. It stands on its nest and flaps its wings. In only three weeks, it flutters toward the ground on one of its first flights. A week later, it can fly in any direction.

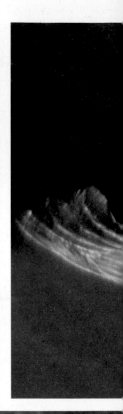

AMERICAN ROBIN (ABOVE), SNOW GOOSE (BELOW)

Baby geese hatch in nests on the ground. They learn to fly by running and flapping their wings. Soon these goslings will be able to take off.

By flying, birds can find food and escape from enemies. What helps birds to fly? Feathers do. Birds are the only animals that have feathers.

OSTRICH (ABOVE), HUMBOLDT PENGUIN (BELOW)

16

KIWI

Some birds cannot fly. Ostriches
are the world's largest birds. They
can run faster than most other
animals, but they do not fly.
A penguin uses its wings as flippers
to swim. The kiwi cannot fly either.
It nests in the ground, and
only comes out at night.

Spring is mating time for most birds.
A male and a female grebe dance
through the water to attract each
other, calling loudly. To find a mate,
a male sparrow sings and sings.
A tern offers his mate a tasty fish.
Together, they will look for a place to
build their nest and start their family.

Birds build nests in many different places. A stork has made its huge nest on top of a chimney. Unlike most other birds, the stork returns to the same home every year. Look carefully at this wren's nest. He has used string in it. A goose lines her nest on the ground with down. These soft feathers from her body will make it comfortable and keep her eggs warm.

FAIRY BLUE WREN

WHITE STORK (OPPOSITE), CANADA GOOSE (ABOVE)

Nests are made of many things that birds find. But all nests are places for birds to care for their eggs and their young.

CLIFF SWALLOW (BELOW AND OPPOSITE)

Cliff swallows live in large groups called colonies. Sometimes they make their round homes under the roofs of buildings or under cliffs. Back and forth the swallow flies, gathering mud. With its mouth, it rolls the mud into tiny balls and sticks row after row together. Where Adélie penguins live, they have only stones to use in building a nest. Then the female lays one or two eggs in it. When the chicks hatch, both parents help take care of them.

ADÉLIE PENGUIN

MASKED WEAVER BIRD

A bird called a limpkin stands on its nest floating on the water in a marsh. It made the nest of plants that grow here. Above the water, the limpkin's eggs are safe from many enemies. The male weaver bird works hard weaving a nest of grass to attract a mate. The female looks over the finished nest carefully. If she does not like it, the male tears it apart and starts all over!

LIMPKIN

LEAST TERN

Birds' eggs need special care. A flamingo gently turns her egg. A tern warms speckled eggs in a nest on the ground. The king penguin does not build a nest. Instead, the egg is kept on top of the parent's feet, under a fold of skin. Here it is protected until it hatches.

GREATER FLAMINGO (OPPOSITE), KING PENGUIN (ABOVE)

CARDINAL

Once the baby birds hatch, the parents are very busy. Cardinals beg from their mother as she watches over them.

Baby birds eat and eat. These hummingbirds are almost as large as their parents, but they still must be cared for. Hungry flickers poke their heads out for more food. Their parents keep them safe in their home in a tree hole.

BROAD-TAILED HUMMINGBIRD (ABOVE), YELLOW-SHAFTED FLICKER (OPPOSITE)

Goslings stay between their parents as they paddle across a lake. Like all baby birds, they will grow up quickly.

CANADA GOOSE

Someday they will have families of their own to raise.
Aren't you glad you can find birds living all around you?

*Published by* The National Geographic Society
Gilbert M. Grosvenor, *President*
Melvin M. Payne, *Chairman of the Board*
Owen R. Anderson, *Executive Vice President*
Robert L. Breeden, *Vice President,*
  *Publications and Educational Media*

*Prepared by* The Special Publications Division
Donald J. Crump, *Director*
Philip B. Silcott, *Associate Director*
William L. Allen, William R. Gray, *Assistant Directors*

*Staff for this Book*
Merrill Windsor, *Managing Editor*
Jim Abercrombie, *Picture Editor*
Cynthia B. Scudder, *Art Director*
Marianne R. Koszorus, *Consulting Art Director*
Monica P. Bradsher, *Consulting Editor*
Brooke Jennings Kane, *Researcher*
Carol A. Rocheleau, *Illustrations Assistant*
Nancy F. Berry, Pamela A. Black, Mary Frances Brennan,
  Mary Elizabeth Davis, Rosamund Garner, Victoria D.
  Garrett, Rebecca Bittle Johns, Virginia W. McCoy, Cleo E.
  Petroff, Tammy Presley, Sheryl A. Prohovich, Kathleen T.
  Shea, *Staff Assistants*

*Engraving, Printing, and Product Manufacture*
Robert W. Messer, *Manager*
George V. White, *Production Manager*
Mary A. Bennett, *Production Project Manager*
Mark R. Dunlevy, Richard A. McClure, David V. Showers,
  Gregory Storer, *Assistant Production Managers*
Katherine H. Donohue, *Senior Production Assistant*
Julia F. Warner, *Production Staff Assistant*

*Consultants*
Dr. Glenn O. Blough, *Educational Consultant*
Lynda Ehrlich, *Reading Consultant*
Frank Y. Larkin, *Scientific Consultant*

*Illustrations Credits*
Jane Burton/BRUCE COLEMAN INC. (cover, 2 upper left, 2 center, 2 lower, 3); Jen & Des Bartlett (1, 6 lower, 8-9, 14-15 lower, 16-17, 23 lower left, 23 lower right, 24, 27 lower); Ron Austing (4-5); M. P. Kahl (5, 19 lower, 20, 22, 27 upper); Lynn M. Stone (6 upper); Gary Nuechterlein (7, 18-19); ANIMALS ANIMALS/Margot Conte (8 upper); Dwight R. Kuhn (9 upper, 14 upper, 19 upper); Lynn Rogers (10-11); William J. Weber (12 upper, 12 lower); Alan Strange and Doug Wilson (12-13); ANIMALS ANIMALS/Michael Habicht (14-15 center, 15 upper); Jen & Des Bartlett/BRUCE COLEMAN INC. (16 lower); M. F. Soper/BRUCE COLEMAN INC. (17 lower); Constance Warner (21 upper); ANIMALS ANIMALS/Breck P. Kent (21 lower); Len Rue, Jr./LEONARD RUE ENTERPRISES (22-23); Stan Osolinski (24-25); ANIMALS ANIMALS/David C. Fritts (26); Alvin E. Staffan (28 upper); Joe Branney/AMWEST (28 lower); ANIMALS ANIMALS/Ralph A. Reinhold (29); ANIMALS ANIMALS/Charles Palek (30-31); Hal H. Harrison/GRANT HEILMAN PHOTOGRAPHY (32); Chip Clark (front and back endpapers).

**Library of Congress CIP Data**

McCauley, Jane R., 1947-
  Baby birds and how they grow.

  (Books for young explorers)
  Summary: Pictures and text introduce various birds in different stages of caring for their eggs and their young.
  1. Birds—Eggs and nests—Juvenile literature.
  2. Birds—Development—Juvenile literature.
  3. Animals, Infancy of—Juvenile literature. [1. Birds—Eggs and nests. 2. Birds—Development. 3. Animals—Infancy] I. Title. II. Series.

QL675.M5 1983                         598.256                         83-13150
ISBN 0-87044-487-5 (regular edition)
ISBN 0-87044-492-1 (library edition)

*Cover:* Just a day after hatching, mallard ducklings swim and walk among the leaves of a water lily.
*Endpapers:* Birds' eggs come in many sizes, shapes, and colors. Here we show 16 different eggs, each about ¾ actual size.

BLACK-CAPPED CHICKADEE

Young chickadees wait in line for a meal from mother. But both parents share in feeding, as well as building the nest and warming the eggs.

Ostrich

Chicken

Laughing
Gull —

Killdeer

Great
Horned
Owl

Robin

Greater Masked
Weaver